# Hidden in the Snow

## Barbara Taylor

QED Publishing

Project Editor: Angela Royston
Designer: Matthew Kelly
Picture Researcher: Maria Joannou

**Front cover:** A baby seal hides on the bumpy ice that covers the Arctic Ocean.

Copyright © QED Publishing 2011

First published in the UK in 2011 by
QED Publishing
A Quarto Group Company
226 City Road
London EC1V 2TT
www.qed-publishing.co.uk

The words in **bold** are explained in the Glossary on page 22.

ISBN  978 1 84835 602 3

Printed in China

**Picture credits**
(t=top, b=bottom, l=left, r=right, fc=front cover, bc=back cover)
**Alamy** Alaska Stock LLC fc; **Corbis** Andrew Parkinson 15b, Wayne Lynch/All Canada Photos 21b; **FLPA** Michio Hoshino/Minden Pictures 4, Konrad Wothe/Minden Pictures 5l, Tom Vezo/Minden Pictures 5r, Michael Quinton/Minden Pictures 7t, Jurgen & Christine Sohns/ 1, 12, Reinhard Hölzl/Imagebroker 13l, Patricio Robles Gil/Minden Pictures 14, Michael Quinton/Minden Pictures 15t, Franz Christoph Robi/ Imagebroker 16, Hiroya Minakuchi/Minden Pictures 17r, Tui De Roy/Minden Pictures 18, Jim Brandenburg/ Minden Pictures 21t; **Nature Picture Library** Chris Gomersall 6, Staffan Widstrand 8, Steven Kazlowski 11, Doug Perrine 17l, Pete Cairns 20; **Photolibrary** Doug Allan 7b, J-L. Klein & M-L. Hubert 9, Peter Arnold Images 10, AlaskaStock 13r, Peter Arnold Images/Gerard Lacz 19; **Shutterstock** Jan Martin Will bc, Hunter 2/3, Lizard 22-23, Armin Rose 24.

# Contents

# Hiding in the Snow

Animals that live in cold, snowy places are good at hide and seek. The animals hide by blending in with their background. This is called **camouflage**.

Some animals are white to match the snow and ice on the ground. Baby harp seals have white fur. They are born on the ice and have to stay there until they grow up.

▲ Baby harp seals keep very still so that polar bears and other hunters will not see them.

4

## Rocky ground

Other animals, such as gyrfalcons, live in places where rocks show through the snow. They have brown, grey and white patterns to match the brown and grey rocks.

▲ A gyrfalcon flies close to the ground. It is looking for prey.

## ANIMAL TALK

- Animals that hunt and kill other animals for food are called **predators**.

- The animals that they hunt are called **prey**.

▶ The Arctic wolf is a predator. Its pale fur matches the white snow.

# As white as snow

The coldest places on Earth are at the tops of high mountains and in the **Arctic** and **Antarctic**. White ice and snow cover the land and much of the sea.

Many animals have white fur or feathers. A snow petrel's white feathers help to hide it from predators such as skuas, which are larger sea birds.

sharp eyes for spotting fish in the sea

white feathers ⟩

▲ A snow petrel is about the same size as a pigeon.

## Mountain sheep

Dall sheep live wild on snowy mountains. In winter, the sheep move down the mountains to keep warm. Wolves and other hungry hunters try to catch them, but the white sheep vanish like ghosts in the snow.

curved horn ····▶

▶ Dall sheep live on very steep mountain slopes, where predators find it hard to chase after them.

rough pads on feet for gripping slippery slopes ····▶

**HIDE AND SEEK**

How many snow petrels can you count in the photo below?

# Hunting in the Snow

Predators need to get close to their prey. This makes it easier for them to catch a meal. Hunted animals can run very fast and may escape before they are caught.

Arctic wolves are white, like the snow around them. Wolves hunt together in groups, called **packs**. It is hard for the animals they hunt to spot all the wolves. Some wolves can get close to the prey without being seen.

▶ Arctic wolves blend in with the snow as they hunt for prey.

## Snow leopards

Snow leopards have grey fur with dark grey circles, which make them almost invisible among the grey mountain rocks where they live.

A snow leopard **stalks** its prey. It slowly creeps closer, keeping as quiet as possible. If the animal it is hunting looks up, the leopard keeps very still, so the prey cannot see it.

- A pack of wolves can catch an animal much larger than themselves.

- Snow leopards cannot roar. They purr instead.

thick fur for keeping warm

long tail to help the leopard keep its balance

# Great white bears

Polar bears are the biggest white animals in the world. Polar bears hunt for seals, which usually swim under the ice that covers the sea in winter.

Seals make holes in the ice so they can come up for air. The polar bear waits next to a seal's breathing hole. The bear's white fur camouflages it from the seal.

▼ A polar bear lies very still as it waits for a seal to pop its head out to breathe in air.

## Surprise attack

The polar bear pounces on the seal and drags it out of the water. Then the bear bites the seal to kill it before starting to feed. Afterwards, the bear cleans its fur by swimming in the water or rolling in the snow.

rough, furry soles on paws for gripping the ice

thick fur and thick fat for keeping warm

▲ A polar bear rolls in the snow to clean its fur. Polar bears don't feel the cold!

# Hiding from hunters

Hunted animals use camouflage, too. Many of these animals are small and weak. Hiding from a scary predator is one of the best ways to stay alive.

Snowshoe hares often live in groups. If a predator comes near, the hares keep really still so they are hard to see. But if the hunter gets too close, the hares scatter. Then the hunter can't decide which hare it should follow!

three layers of fur for keeping warm

big furry feet to stop the snowshoe hare sinking into the snow

long, thick
fur

## No camouflage!

Marmots have grey-brown fur, which blends with the rocks in summer. They don't need white camouflage, because they sleep in **burrows** right through the snowy winter.

Musk oxen do not need white camouflage in winter either. Adult musk oxen are so big, with such big **horns**, no animal attacks them.

horn

◄ This marmot is keeping a look out for predators, such as a fox or eagle.

► Adult musk oxen use their big horns to defend their young.

## ANIMAL TALK

- Marmots spend eight months a year asleep in their deep burrows.

- Musk oxen form a circle around their young calves to protect them from wolves.

13

# Babies and chicks

Baby animals are small and can't defend themselves. Babies are always hungry and need a lot to eat! They are often left alone while their parents go off to find food for them.

Reindeer **calves** are only as big as a hare when they are born in summer. Their plain, brown fur blends in well with the brown ground. It helps to keep them safe from hunters such as wolves.

- One-day-old reindeer calves can run faster than a person.

- An eider duck pulls out her own fluffy feathers to line her nest and keep her eggs warm.

▲ Baby reindeer have long legs so that they can run fast and keep up with the rest of the herd.

## Mothers and chicks

There are few trees in very cold places, so most birds make their nests on the ground. Female birds usually sit on the nest to keep their eggs warm, so they need to be well camouflaged.

▲ This Arctic tern chick and egg are both well camouflaged.

▲ These eider ducklings follow their mother wherever she goes.

# Light and dark

Many animals that live in cold oceans have light tummies and dark backs. These colours hide them when they are seen from below or above.

Puffins dive underwater to catch fish. When the fish look up from below, they find it hard to see the white bellies of the puffins against the light sky. But if a predator above looks down, the puffin's black back disappears against the dark water.

white belly and breast ·······>

webbed feet for swimming ·······>

◀ Puffins can swim underwater as well as fly in the air.

## Orcas

An orca's light and dark patterns hide it in a different way. Patches of light and dark flicker below the sea. When it is seen from the side, the orca disappears against this background.

### ANIMAL TALK

- Puffins are sometimes called sea parrots because of their colourful bills.
- An orca is a type of dolphin.

▼ Orcas live and hunt in groups called pods.

flippers for steering

wide tail for swimming

# Penguin patterns

Penguins have a black back and a white tummy to camouflage them when they are swimming in the sea.

From above, the penguin's black back merges with the dark water. From below, its white tummy blends in with the lighter surface of the sea.

▲ The penguin's camouflage helps it to catch food and to escape from sharks and other hunters.

## Keeping warm

Black things soak up heat better than white things do. The penguin's black back soaks up the heat of the sun. This helps the penguin to warm up after being in the icy sea.

strong beak for gripping slippery fish

smooth top feathers for keeping out the water

fluffy feathers underneath for keeping warm

▲ Different types of penguin are different colours and have different patterns.

19

# Changing colour

Some animals have white fur in winter. Then it changes to brown fur in summer! Their fur changes colour to match the colour of the ground around them.

In winter, snow covers the ground. The Arctic fox's coat of white fur is hard to see against the snow. Its white fur is very thick and keeps the fox warm in winter.

◄ White fur helps an Arctic fox to get close to its prey.

## Summertime

In summer, the snow melts and the ground is covered with brown and grey rocks. The Arctic fox's fur coat changes from white to brown to match the rocks.

To change colour, furry animals lose their old fur and grow new fur in its place. This happens as the weather becomes warmer.

## HIDE AND SEEK

The Arctic fox hunts Arctic hares, which also change colour in winter and summer. How many Arctic hares can you spot in the photo above?

big ears for hearing prey under the ground

◀ This fox has some of its white winter fur and some of its brown summer fur.

21

# Glossary

**Antarctic** The frozen continent around the South Pole.

**Arctic** The frozen ocean and very cold lands around the North Pole.

**burrow** A long tunnel dug in the soil by animals such as marmots.

**calf** The young of many different animals including reindeer, whales and seals.

**camouflage** Colours, patterns or markings that help an animal to hide by matching the background.

**horn** A hard growth on the head of a hoofed animal. Horns are often pointed or curved, but they do not branch out.

**pack** A group of hunting animals, such as wolves.

**predator** An animal that hunts and kills other animals for food.

**prey** An animal hunted and killed by a predator.

**stalk** The slow and silent way in which a hunter carefully creeps up on its prey.

**Did you spot them all?**
How many animals did you count in the Hide and Seek photos? Did you spot four snow petrels on page 7 and eight Arctic hares on page 21? The better the animals are camouflaged, the harder they are to spot!

# Index

# Notes for parents and teachers

As you share this book with children, ask questions to encourage them to look closely at the detail in the photographs.

## What is snow?

- Explain to the children what snow is. Snow is made up of delicate crystals of ice, with air between them. Light reflected from these crystals makes the snow sparkle and look white.
- Help the children make paper snowflakes and explore symmetry.
- Talk about the feel of snow – its fluffy texture, its lightness and its coldness – and how it melts and freezes into ice when it is pressed together in a snowball. Have the children ever made a snowman or a snow hare?

## Moving around

- Camouflage works best when animals keep still, but they have to move sometimes!
- Ask the children to play camouflage hide and seek. Each child can pick a surface or area they want to blend into and then dress up to match it, for example a white bed sheet in front of a white wall. After the game is finished, the children can vote for their favourite costume and discuss who was the most camouflaged.

## Hunters and hunted

- Look through the book and ask the children to find the predators (hunters) and the prey (hunted animals). This can be different from one page to the next, as many predators are prey for larger animals! Make a collage of a food chain. Show, for example, an Arctic wolf hunting an Arctic fox, and an Arctic fox hunting an Arctic hare, which eats plants.

## Keeping warm

- Explain how several layers of fur or feathers trap pockets of air. These retain an animal's body heat.
- Because people don't have thick fur like animals, we need to wear warm clothing in winter. Ask the children how they stay warm when it's cold outside.

## Changing colour

- Tell the children that fur and feathers are dead structures, so mammals and birds can't change their colour straight away.
- Animals that change colour with the seasons grow a whole new coat of fur or feathers. This is called moulting. Can the children remember which animals change colours?